This Hair Belongs

THIS HAIR BELONGS

JaNay Brown-Wood   Illustrated by Erin K. Robinson

ASTRA YOUNG READERS

AN IMPRINT OF ASTRA BOOKS FOR YOUNG READERS
New York

This hair
grew
from the scalps of kings and queens,

each curly strand standing tall
as if reaching for the sun beneath opulent crowns.

This hair
waves
like rivers that span Africa's grand lands—
Zambezi, Congo, Niger;

t spirals
like winds blowing desert sands of the
Namib, Kalahari, Sahara.

This hair
curls
like the corkscrew albuca;
it spans
generations long like the church in Ethiopia
and the pyramids of Egypt.

This hair shrinks
like the unspun cotton of kente.
It stretches
like the banks of the Nile.

This hair is magic.

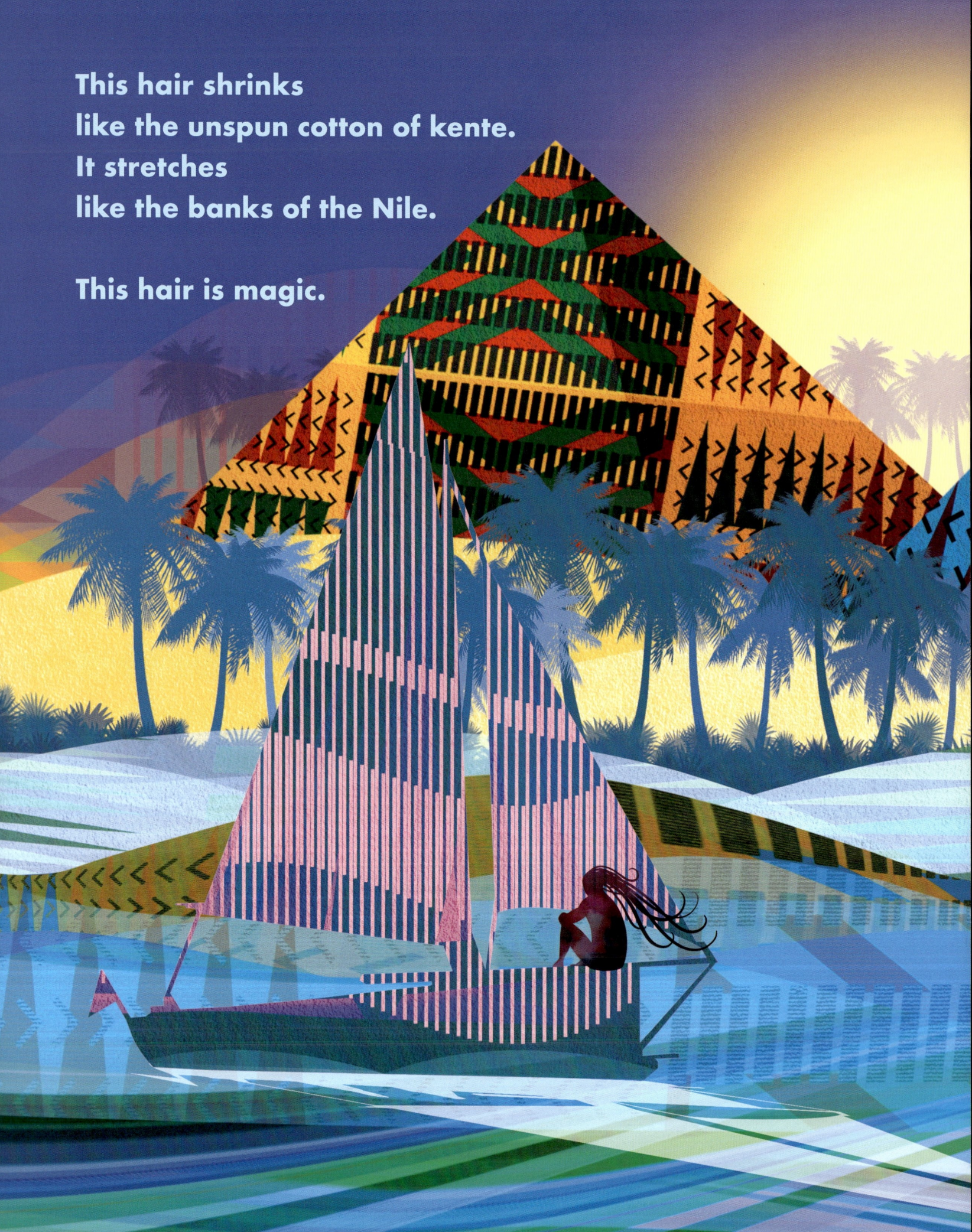

While it might be thick, thick it is
known that
this hair
protected the skin atop our ancestors'
heads.

While it may tangle, tangle it is told
that
this hair
hid grains and seeds later planted to
grow and fill our ancestors' bellies.

While it might stick out, stick up it is clear that this hair
yielded to creative, nimble fingers
perfecting our ancestors' designs.

While it may knot, knot it is relayed that this hair
held secret messages guiding our ancestors' ways.

This hair
is who we are.
We are
Black
and
Beautiful
and
Proud.
And our hair is magic.

When our hair was shaved
 and ridiculed
  and likened to the wool of uncouth beasts—
 we lost our way.

  But hair like this will not be tamed,
  will not be hidden,
  will not be shamed,
   will not be forgotten or lose its way
   forever.

The roots of
this hair
grow deep.

This hair is magic. This hair belongs.

Twisted, braided, dreaded, faded. Straightened, cornrowed, froed and plaited. Beaded, flattened, or tied up tight.

THIS HAIR BELONGS.

THIS HAIR IS MAGIC.

This hair belongs
in the past, the now, the future,
in the real and the imagined,
in the myth and in the legend.

This hair belongs under the sea,
in outer space, in shires and realms
and woods and kingdoms.

THIS.
HAIR
IS. MAGIC.
THIS.
HAIR
BELONGS.

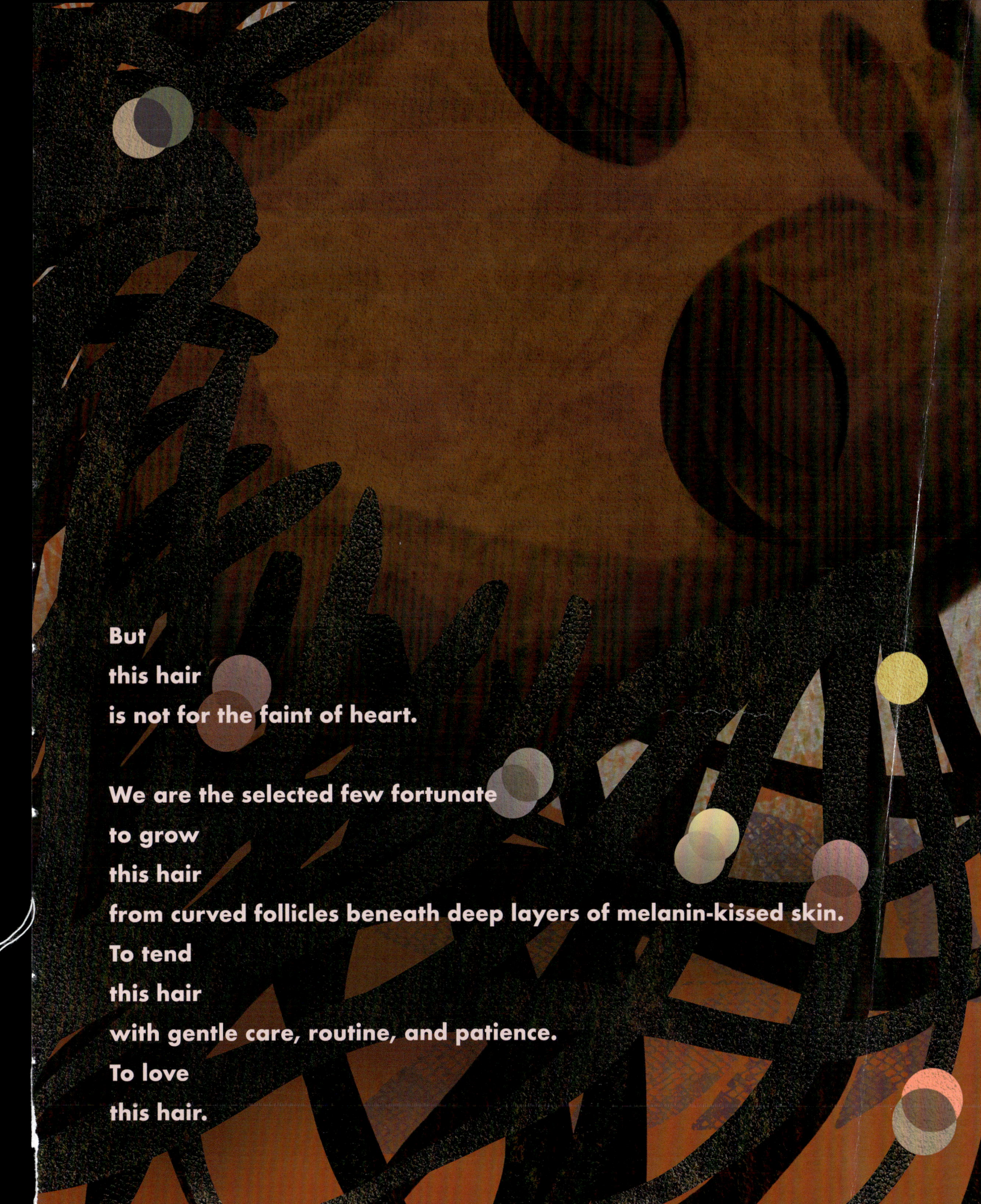

But
this hair
is not for the faint of heart.

We are the selected few fortunate
to grow
this hair
from curved follicles beneath deep layers of melanin-kissed skin.
To tend
this hair
with gentle care, routine, and patience.
To love
this hair.

This hair is black gold. This hair is a crown.
Your hair is black gold. Your hair is a crown.

Hold it up high
for the history
it holds.

For your people.
For you.

You are magic.
And you belong.

AUTHOR'S NOTE

My hair was chemically relaxed for most of my childhood. I have memories of sitting in a chair, having my hair be parted into sections, and then a thick cream being brushed on, bit by bit. I remember the cream burning—like fire or acid—and even leaving wounds on my scalp. I endured this treatment until I was an adult, when I finally embraced my natural hair. I can recall—as a thirty-year-old woman—looking in the mirror, pulling one of my curls and being astonished. I had never really looked at the natural kink of my hair before, did not even realize how it curls in perfect spirals. Now, I wear my hair naturally, either braided, twisted, or styled in different ways.

This acceptance of my own hair has not been an easy process—especially since Black hair is stigmatized in society. There are countless examples of Black adults and children being scorned for wearing their hair naturally—so much so that laws had to be passed to stop discrimination against wearing natural hair in professional settings. Specifically, the CROWN Act was introduced in my home state of California and passed in 2019. The US Congress passed the CROWN Act in 2021 to protect against hairstyle or hair texture discrimination.

I wish I'd had a book like this one when I was a young girl. Perhaps it would have helped me embrace my natural hair sooner. But I am honored to share this book today with hopes that the young readers who see themselves in my words and in Erin's illustrations, will internalize that YES, their hair is magic and that they—and all their beauty and gifts and Blackness—belong.

A GLIMPSE OF AFRICAN HISTORY AND HAIR

KINGS AND QUEENS OF AFRICA

Throughout African history, kings and queens ruled over the lands, including prominent royalty such as Amenhotep III of ancient Egypt (thirteenth and fourteenth centuries BCE); Nefertiti the Queen of ancient Egypt (fourteenth century BCE); Makeda the Queen of Sheba (tenth century BCE); and Mansa Musa of Mali (fourteenth century CE). African kings and queens wore different types of headdresses, ranging from ornate wraps to headpieces adorned in gold and beads, atop their beautiful, natural hair.

THE NILE AND OTHER RIVERS OF AFRICA

Africa has many, many rivers weaving across its continent and throughout its more than fifty countries and five regions (North, East, West, South, and Central). The Nile is not only the longest river in Africa—followed by the Congo, Niger, and Zambezi—but it is the longest river in the whole world! It is about 4,132 miles long, flowing through eleven African countries beginning at Lake Victoria and gushing into the Mediterranean Sea.

DESERTS OF AFRICA (AND WIND WITHIN THEM)

Africa is the home of many large deserts, which are hot, dry places that do not receive much rainfall. The Sahara is the largest desert on the continent and is about the size of mainland United States. The Sahara also experiences major dust storms called haboobs. Haboobs happen in dry, arid places because of strong thunderstorm winds, which can create walls of dust that whip through the land.

CORKSCREW ALBUCA

The *Albuca spiralis*, also known as the corkscrew albuca or the frizzle sizzle, is a plant originating in South Africa. The thin leaves of the plant grow inward at the tips, like a spiral, and the plant produces a greenish-yellowish flower.

CHURCHES IN ETHIOPIA

Christian beliefs span back many centuries and in the fourth century CE, Ethiopia was one of the first countries to embrace Christianity. In the late twelfth and early thirteenth centuries, King Lalibela constructed eleven churches that were each carved from a single volcanic rock. These Ethiopian churches still stand today, including the Biete Mariam (House of Mary) and the cross-shaped Biete Ghiorgis (House of Saint George). The rock churches of Lalibela are so treasured that they have been declared World Heritage sites by the United Nations Educational, Scientific and Cultural Organization (UNESCO), an international organization that identifies, protects, and preserves property and possessions of cultural or natural importance.

PYRAMIDS OF EGYPT

Pyramids are structures built out of materials such as bricks or stone with a wide base and a point at the top. Ancient Egyptians built pyramids (such as the famous Pyramids of Giza) as tombs, often to memorialize past pharaohs. However, pyramids can be found throughout Africa, including in Sudan and Ethiopia.

KENTE CLOTH

African clothing is known for its bright colors and designs. Kente is a type of cloth originating in Ghana, made from silk and cotton thread. In the past, the cotton was harvested, deseeded, smoothed, stretched, and spun into thread, then dyed. The threads were woven using a loom and African techniques to make the cloth. This whole process was done by hand, but today, some of the process has been replaced by machines and factories.

PURPOSE OF HAIR

Hair has served many purposes across history using braided designs. But the main biological purpose of human hair is to protect the skin from the environment like the sun and its ultraviolet rays, cold, rain, and wind. Hair also helps the body maintain a healthy body temperature.

RICE AND SECRET MESSAGES

While it is difficult to verify since much of the histories of enslaved African peoples have been lost, oral stories state that hair designs helped pass on secret messages. Specifically, enslaved people braided visual maps or directions to safety into each other's hair. This information guided them to freedom. Oral lore also chronicles that seeds of rice from the homeland were braided into hair in secret and later planted to grow food to share among the enslaved.

DESIGN AND STYLE OF BLACK HAIR

Black hair has a history of showcasing intricate designs and styles. Identity and individuality are highlighted through hairstyles across genders and utilizing natural dos or chemically treated styles. These hairdos have a broad range including—just to name a few—braids, twists, dreadlocks, afros, cornrows, shaved, fades, twist outs, wash-and-gos, high-top cuts, relaxed, and so on.

DISPARAGING BLACK HAIR

During and after the time of slavery, the hair of Black people has been shamed, caricatured, ridiculed, and even cut off against the will of the individual. It was even compared to that of animals to dehumanize people of African descent.

BLACK PRIDE

Throughout history, African Americans showed pride in their African heritage and ancestry, despite the hardships they have faced and still face today. Black people were especially loud and proud during the 1960s with civil rights demonstrations, the advocacy of important historical figures such as Martin Luther King Jr., Malcolm X, and the Black Panther Party, and even the lyrics of songs like James Brown's 1968 "Say It Loud." Hairstyles such as afros, braids, and dreadlocks gave Black people another way to proudly show their heritage as they held their heads up high.

IN MYTHS, LEGENDS, AND BOOKS

In the past, some legends, myths, and stories for children have featured Black characters such as mermaids and princesses, though these types of stories have not always been easy to find. Unfortunately, that is still the case today in books and on screen. In fact, there have even been instances of backlash when Black characters are included in fantastical stories, such as when Halle Bailey was cast as Ariel in the live-action version of Disney's *The Little Mermaid* (2023). Diverse stories are important to share with readers and viewers everywhere, and there is still a need more of them, even today.

WHAT IS HAIR?

Hair is a collection of dead, keratinized—which means hardened by a protein called keratin—cells that grow out of the scalp skin from a structure called a follicle. The base of the follicle is called a hair bulb, which makes new cells at the bottom of the hair strand that push the rest of the hair upward. This is how hair grows!

MELANIN AND CURL

Hair gets its color from melanin, a substance responsible for giving pigmentation to skin, hair, and the irises of eyes.

For hair, melanin is produced in the hair bulb. As for the curl of hair, the shape and the angle of the bottom part of the follicle impacts whether the hair will grow straight (from round or circle-shaped follicle bases) or have a kink or curl (from oval or elliptical-shaped follicle bases).

BLACK HAIR ROUTINES

Many individuals of African descent engage in hair care routines to maintain their hair, especially since hair tangles and mats if not cared for. Routines include pre-conditioning hair, washing, deep conditioning, detangling, and styling. Also, bedtime routines include twisting or braiding hair, wrapping the head in a head scarf or bonnet, and even sleeping on satin pillowcases. Braiding and twisting the hair are also called protective styles, used to protect the hair and keep it from knotting. Depending on the number of braids and the size of them, these protective styles can take several hours to complete.

To my mother, Marci, my sister Erin, my cousins Denise and Stephanie, and to Peaches, Mishae, Karis, Diana, Lupita Nyong'o, Issa Rae and all the beautiful Black women who helped me care for and embrace my natural hair. —*JB-W*

Is Brooklyn in the house. . . This is for all the magnificent beings of color I've come across who have inspired me to create and represent. —*EKR*

Text copyright © 2026 by JaNay Brown-Wood
Illustrations copyright © 2026 by Erin K. Robinson
All rights reserved. Copying or digitizing this book for storage, display, or distribution in any other medium is strictly prohibited.

For information about permission to reproduce selections from this book, please contact permissions@astrapublishinghouse.com.

Astra Young Readers
An imprint of Astra Books for Young Readers,
a division of Astra Publishing House
astrapublishinghouse.com
Printed in Canada

ISBN: 978-1-6626-2086-7 (hc)
ISBN: 978-1-6626-2087-4 (eBook)
Library of Congress Control Number: 2025935726

Design by Barbara Grzeslo and Michelle Mayhall
The text is set in Futura and Optima LT Std.
The illustrations are done digitally in Procreate.